Opening the Heart

Meditations on How to Be

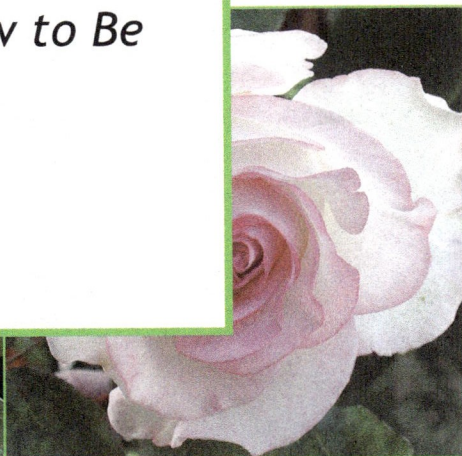

First published by Dog Ear Publishing
4010 W. 86th Street, Ste H
Indianapolis, IN 46268
www.dogearpublishing.net

ISBN: 978-1-4575-2430-1

Book design by Linda M. Lewis

This paper is acid free and meets all ANSI standards for archival quality paper.
Printed in the United States of America

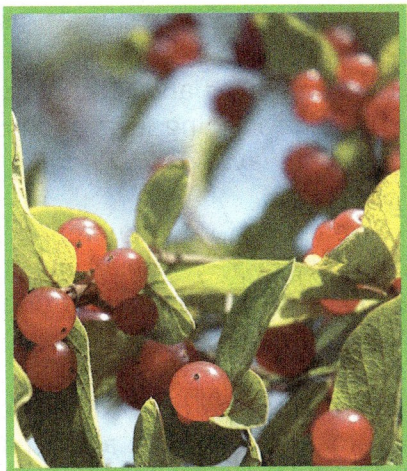

Contents

Introduction

I have been, for a number of years, a spiritual seeker; praying, meditating and reading, sometimes in a more concentrated, mindful way, sometimes hardly at all. At the same time, I was seeking out like-minded people and consulting those I believe to be true intuitives and mediums. I have moved and changed professions, embracing those changes and learning to accept the idea of myself as a life coach and an intuitive. I have been practicing, again sometimes more successfully than others, to live in a mindful and heartful way.

A part of my seeking has led me (along with Linda Lewis) to the creation of these meditation images, meditations and exercises. I hope that these help you, in your own way and time, to find yourself and your path, or reinforce you in the knowledge that you already have. I hope that I have translated well what God, Source, the Divine wants me to give to you.

From early on in the process of bringing *Opening the Heart: Meditations on How to Be* into the world, I knew that one purpose of the meditations was to make us look at and think about the seeming dualities of life, while at the same time learning to perceive the Oneness of existence. This can be seen by looking at the text of the paired meditation images as they came through to me from the Universe, e.g., one image says nature and nurture is on the other image in the pair. Another image is about the quantum nature of the universe, and the accompanying meditation image is about the macrocosmic, seemingly solid nature of things. As I spent time discussing these meditations with my co-creator, Linda Lewis, it became even clearer to me (through her help and wisdom) that another purpose of *Opening the Heart* is to help us think about how we want to live in relation to the divine, the world, our families and friends, and to ourselves.

I find myself in awe of the fact that Linda Lewis immediately committed herself to this project, kept me going through the seemingly slow process, and had me laughing the whole time. But most importantly, she provided wonderful insight and guidance, not only on the graphics and images, but also on the meaning and depth of *Opening the Heart*. I am also awed by the beautiful photographs taken by David Steiner for this project.

I am finding that more people, one by one, are turning away from the categorical rejection of ancient knowledge and ways, as well as the automatic acceptance that all of the modern is worthwhile. The skill of listening to our hearts as well as our minds to find useful knowledge and tools is returning. We are learning the ways that are useful to us to exist spiritually, but also while taking care of the physical, not just our own physical selves, but also Mother Earth and Father Sky, the waters and the land, the animals, the plants. The caveat, of course, is not all of the ancient world should be brought into the modern, and not all of the modern should be rejected. One of our tasks is to find the blend, the harmony, the balance of the ancient and the modern. I believe that *Opening the Heart* can help with this task.

I began leading workshops based on the meditations in *Opening the Heart* while seeking a way to publish the original book and card set. During that process it occurred to me that it would be good for the participants to journal, draw and collage their experiences. As a result, there is some space to begin to do this, especially in the **Notes** section at the end of the book. I feel that that this could be helpful for those who may not be able to attend a workshop or for those who want to continue to work with the exercises. Most of the exercises in Part 3 were created for the workshop or have come to me while thinking about *Opening the Heart* and the workshop. In fact, there are more exercises in this book than can be done in the usual three-hour workshop time frame. Please see **How to Use this Book** for more information.

We are all, in our own ways, persevering in the face of fear generated by those who do not want to see the changes that are coming, do not want to heal, and do not want to live in cooperation but want to keep living in competition. More and more of those with a different vision are speaking about and living a new paradigm. Learning to live in hope and to live from the heart rather than fear is another purpose of *Opening the Heart*.

Listen to your inner self and the Universe, the Divine, and the One. Learn balance, integration and harmony, healing, compassion and gratitude and then be what you are called to be. And, be authentically you. Remember at each moment you are perfect for who you are in the eyes of the Universe. But please also remember that the Universe is all about change, growth and transformation—ours as well as its own.

We and Mother Earth are undergoing a time of shift and transformation. Linda and I recommend *Opening the Heart* as one of the tools that can help us make our own shift and transformation.

How to Use This Book

Part 1 contains the meditation images, which consist of a photograph and text. You can choose one image to contemplate, or you can choose to contemplate both of the paired images. You can contemplate the image with or without reading the meditation text contained in Part 2. Each meditation image is numbered for convenience, making it easier to find the accompanying text. The paired images present a seeming duality of life that can help expand or stretch our thinking and envisioning when meditation is entered into. If you wish to contemplate only one of the paired images, you can place a piece of paper over the other image.

Part 2, as I said previously, contains text to accompany each meditation image in Part 1. The text was created in conjunction with my angels and guides. You can use the text as a trigger for your meditations or you can choose to work only with the meditation images. The information that can come through for you is not limited to the text in this section; however, it can be a place to begin your meditations if you choose.

Part 3 consists of specific exercises to do using the meditation images. Space is provided in Part 3 as a place to begin to journal, draw and/or collage your experience with a particular exercise. The exercises in this section can be done either in one sitting or you can choose to do two or three of the exercises at a time, taking as long as you wish to make your way through all the exercises. You can also do the exercises as a solo experience or in a group. In addition, you can, over time repeat exercises as you are drawn to do them.

The book also contains pages to begin to journal, collage and/or draw in the **Notes** section at the end of the book.

Meditation, for the purpose of both the exercises and the general work with the images, consists of playing music, sitting comfortably with both feet on the floor or lying comfortably, closing your eyes, breathing deeply, and envisioning your heart center opening up. You will hold the intent that meditating on the image will provide you information about the change and transformation that can be yours if you choose it. Envision light entering your heart center if you find this helpful. You can remain in meditation with your eyes closed the entire time while holding the image and text in your mind, or you can open your eyes after entering your heart and meditate on the image that way.

Apart from working with the meditation images and journaling about your experience, you can also choose an image to contemplate over time. Linda and I encourage you to consider buying a bookstand so as to be able to display the image easily whether meditating on it over time or doing a concentrated, specific meditation on it. Another possibility is to choose two or three images to work with at one time. This would consist of choosing one image, writing down the text, then choosing another one, and possibly a third, and doing the same. You would then meditate on the three together to see where this leads you. Or, you can choose three and then meditate on them in succession.

Please choose some meditative music to play while doing the exercises in Part 3 or to help guide you in your meditations while working with the meditation images generally. It should be something that you find enhances the meditation as well as not being distracting.

Once you have completed the meditations, journal, draw and/or collage what you have seen, felt or heard. Again, if you are working in a group, it can be useful to allow anyone who wants to talk about their experience to do so.

Meditation Images

Breathe deeply, breathe slowly.
You can breathe through anything.

1

Action is the counterpart to breath.
Be in the world.

2

Invite the Great Mother
into your heart.

3

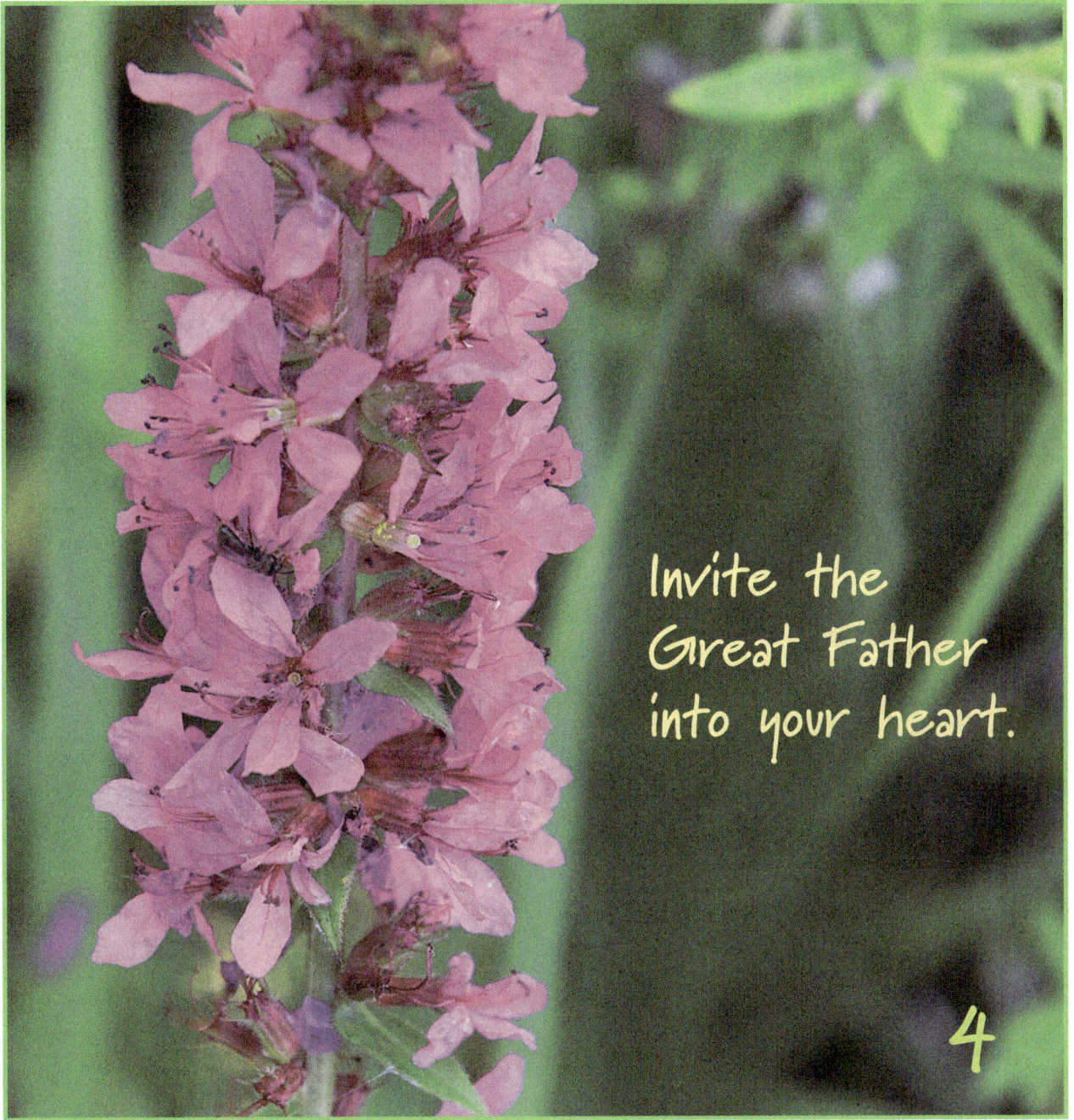

Invite the
Great Father
into your heart.

4

The Holy Spirit invites
you to live your heart
in the world.

5

Holy Wisdom invites
you to enter your
deepest self.

6

Live in your blood and bones.

7

8

Live in your breath.

8

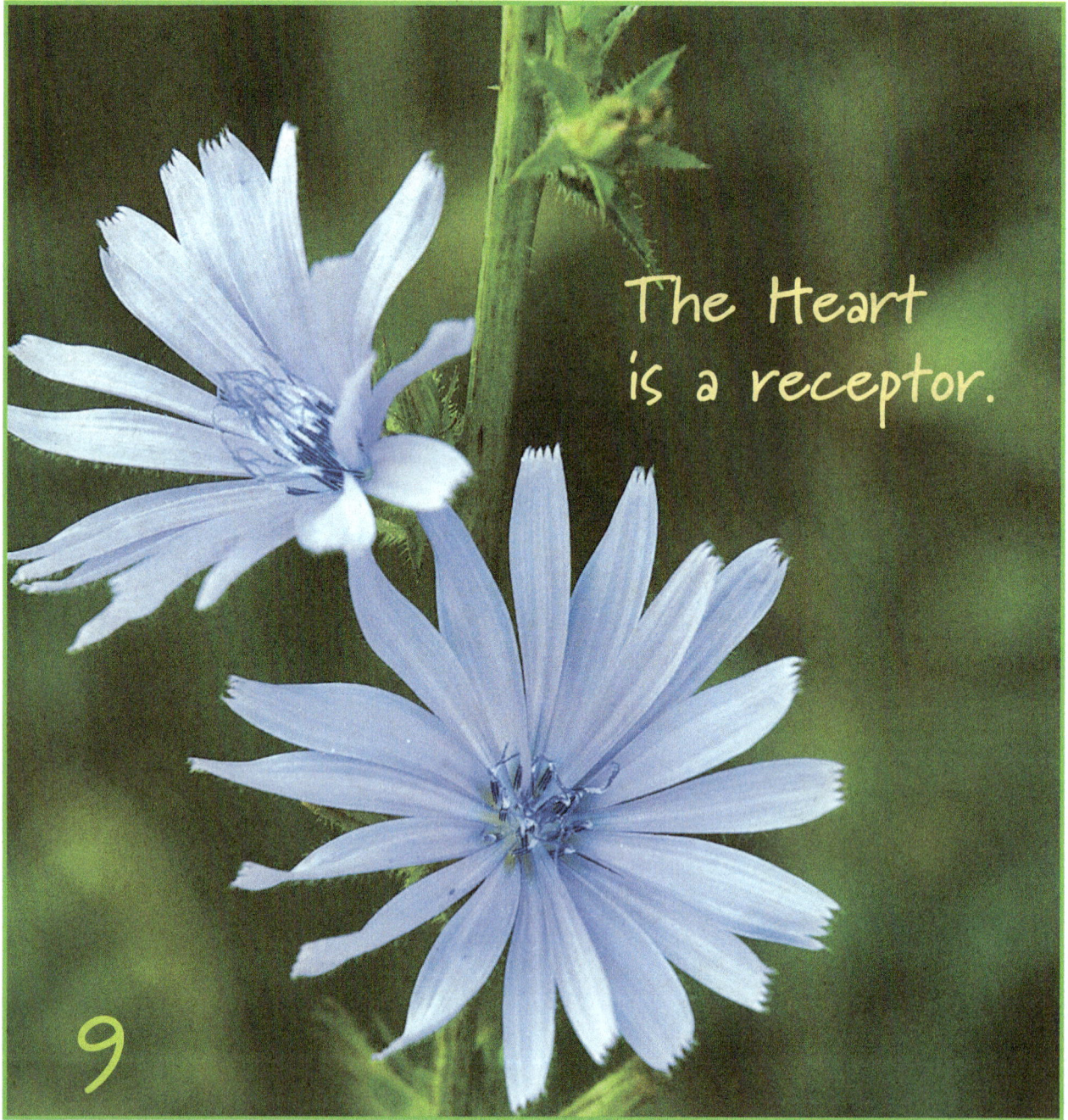

The Heart
is a receptor.

9

10

The Heart is a transmitter.

10

Time does not exist in the heart
of the universe. Be there.

11

Time exists on the
human plane.
Be here.

12

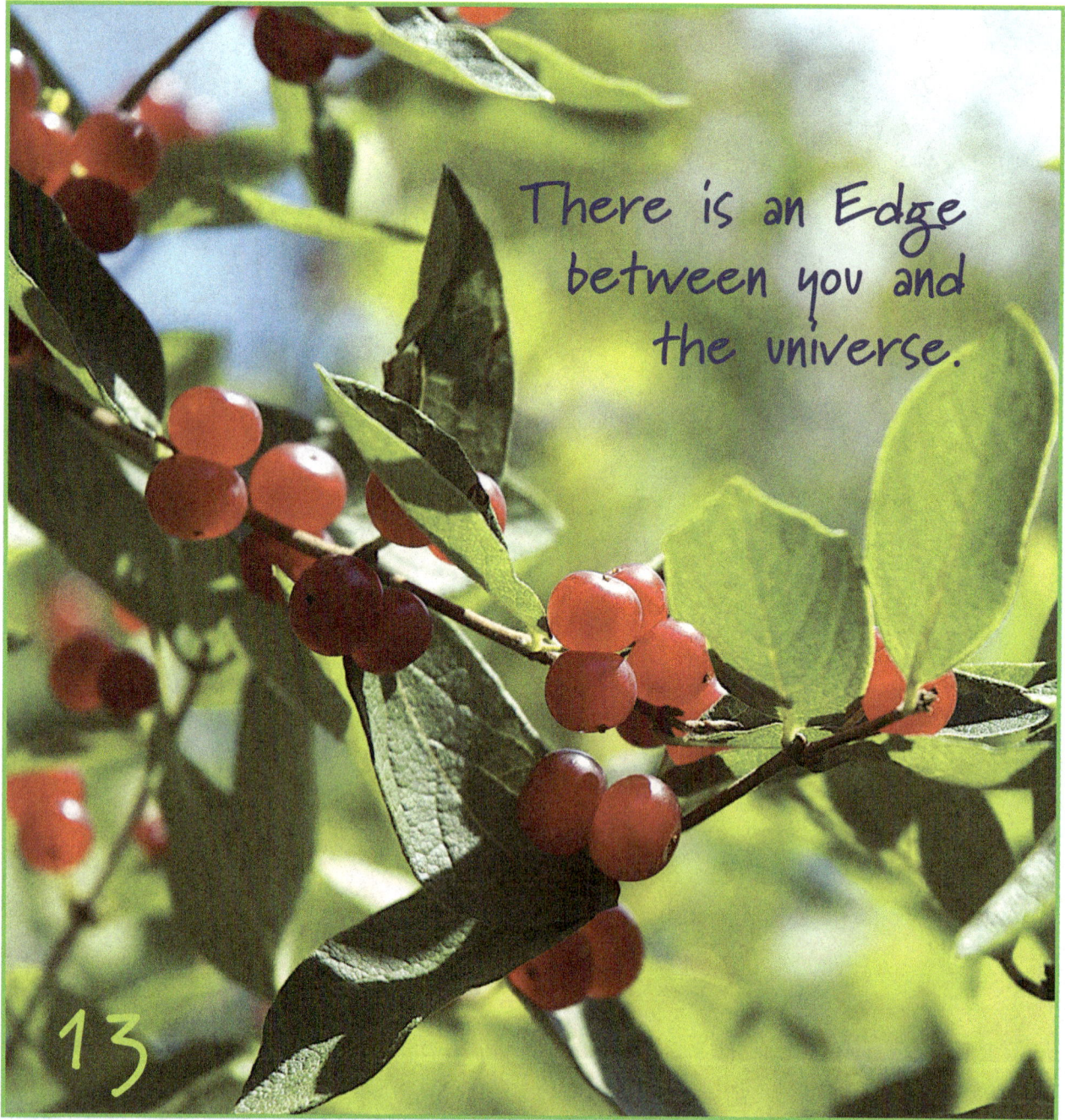

There is an Edge
between you and
the universe.

13

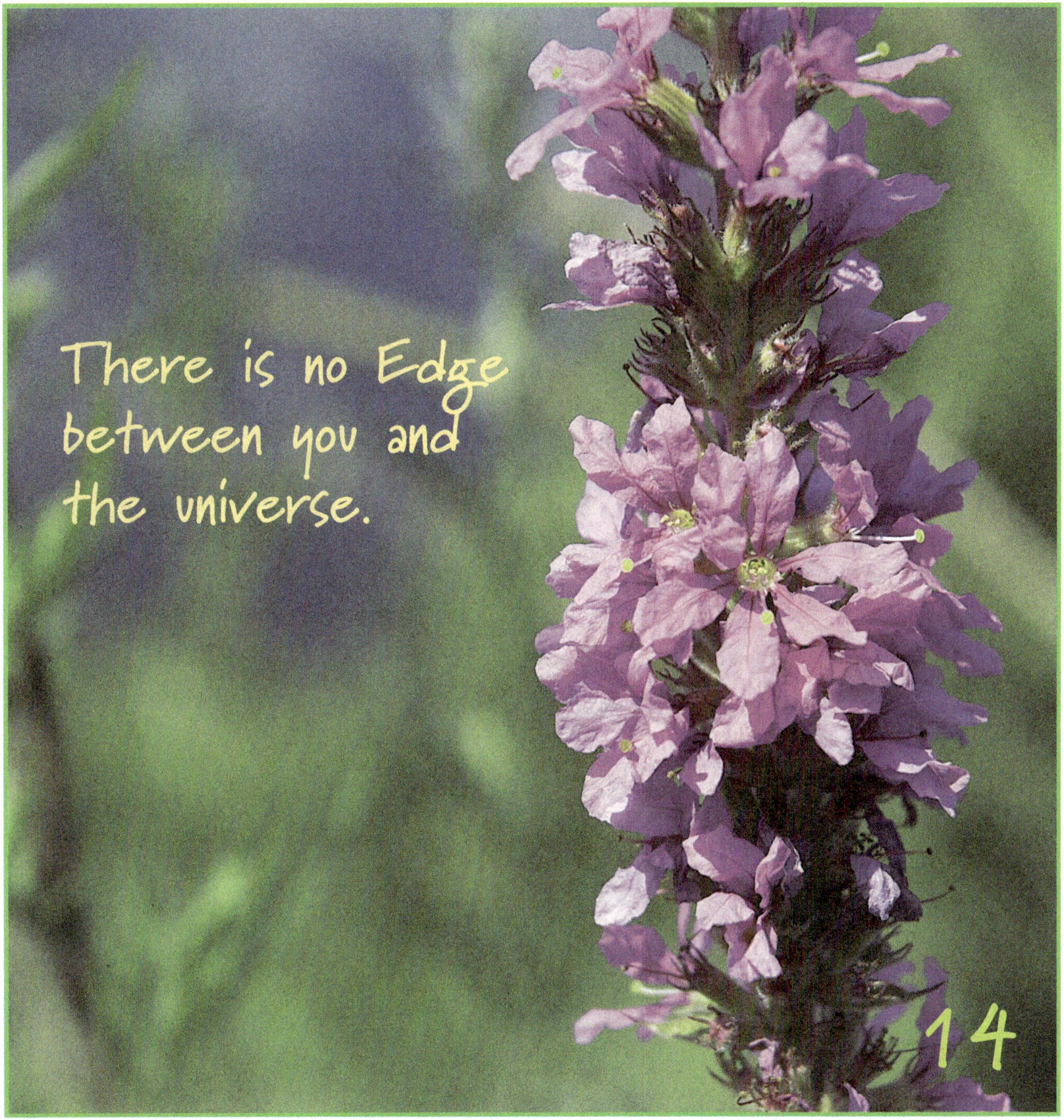
There is no Edge
between you and
the universe.
14

Life is a song.
Sing it.

15

16

Life is a school.
Learn from it.

16

Be open.

17

Have boundaries.

18

Go slowly.
Take your time.

19

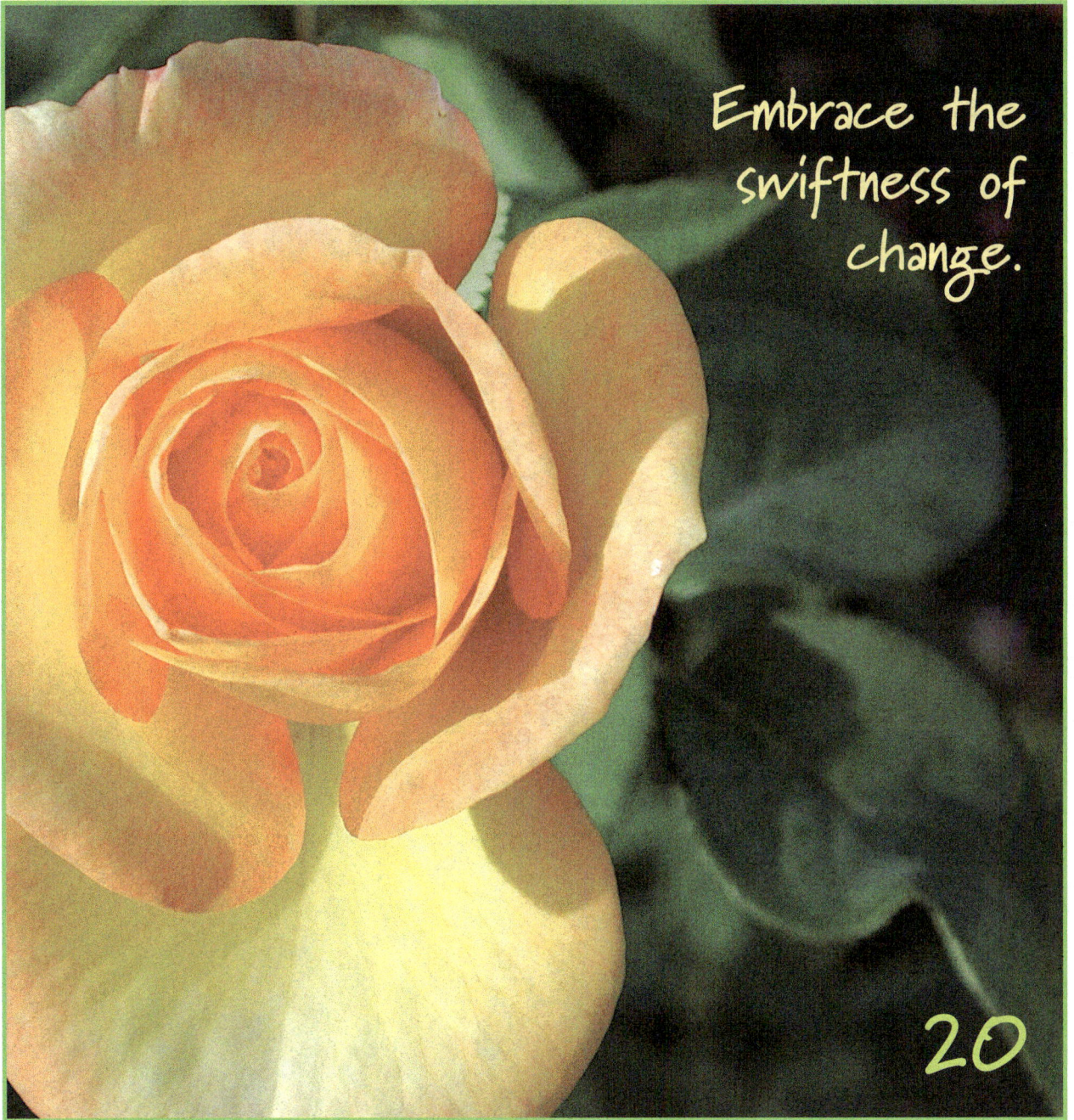

Embrace the swiftness of change.

20

21

Love your country.

Love the world.

22

Accept that you are
called to offer
your best.

23

Accept that sometimes you will fail.

24

The universe
is a quantum
universe.

25

The universe is a
Newtonian universe.

26

Embrace the feminine.

27

Embrace the masculine.

28

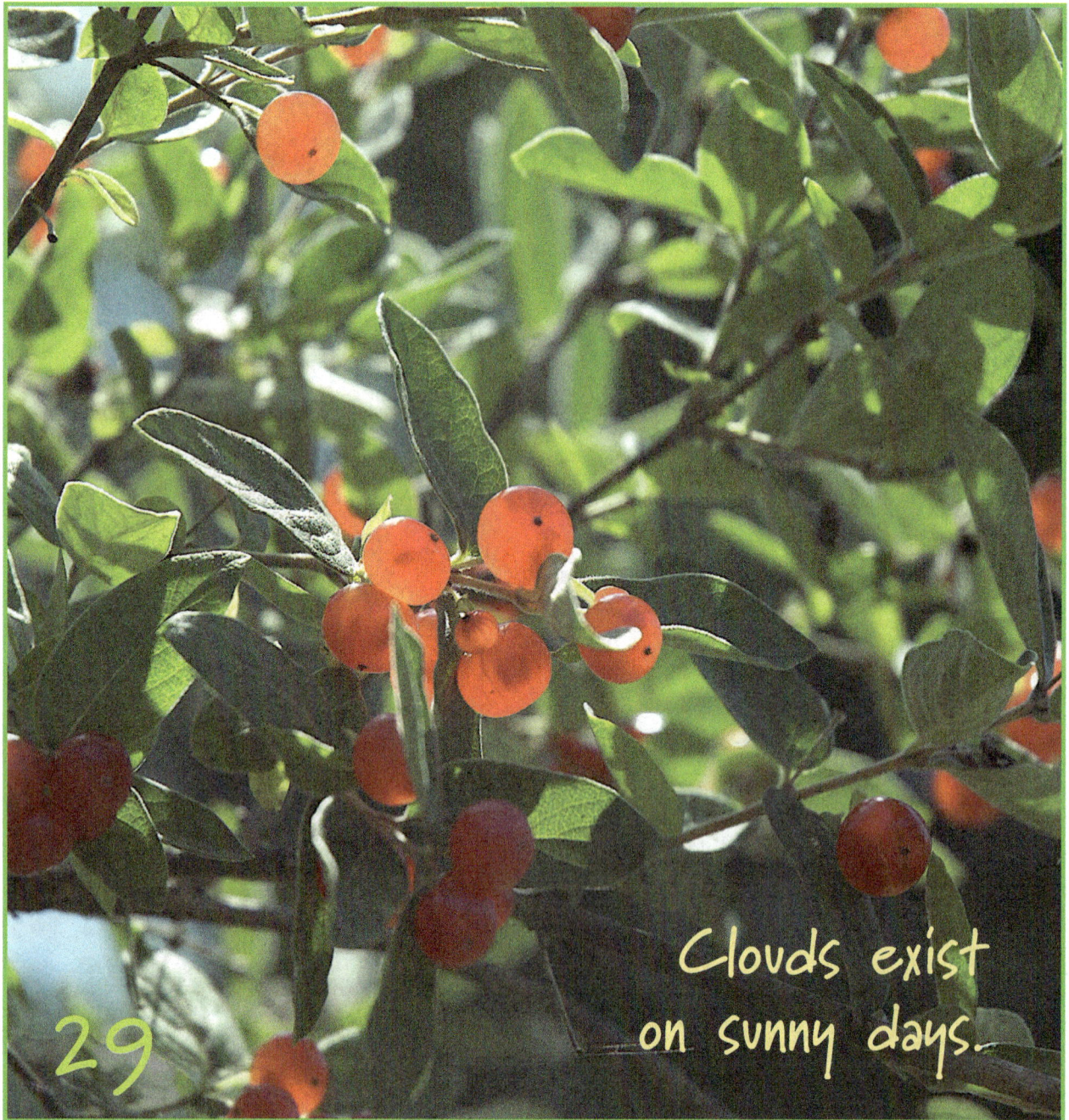

29

Clouds exist
on sunny days.

Bright starlight illuminates the darkest nights.

30

31 Dance your body through life.

Rest your mind in the one.

32

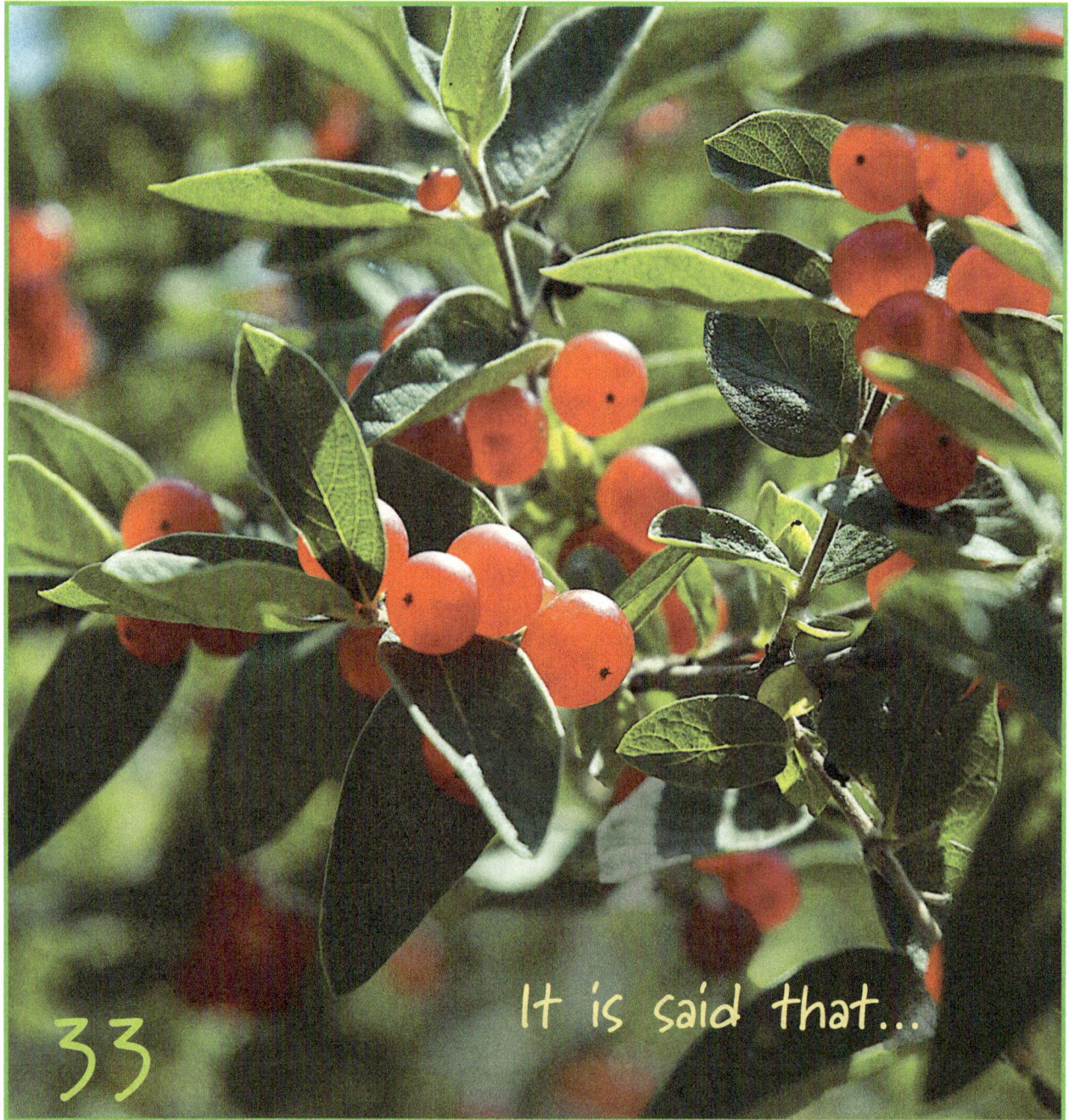

33

It is said that...

34

I know that...

34

Accept and use what ancient wisdom has to give us.

35

Modern wisdom has much to offer.
Use it.

36

It is good to plan
and prepare.

37

It is neccessary to be spontaneous.

38

The earth
is magnificent.
Enjoy it.
Take care of it.

39

The world of
spirit is glorious.
Enjoy it.
Take care of it.

40

Let the nature
of the Elements
support you in
your journey.

41

Let the nature of Mind
guide you in your journey.

42

What you want.

43

What you need.

44

Be playful.

45

Be mindful.

46

Nurture

47

Nature

48

49

In the eyes of the universe,
at this moment, you are
perfect for who you are.

49

Do not stand still.
Do not be static.
Grow. Heal. Change.

50

You are the Beloved.

51

52

You are the one
called to Love.

52

Compassion for others.

53

Compassion for yourself.

54

Let it all go.
It will come
when it
wants to.

55

Seek it.
Seek it in
yourself.

56

Meditations

1 Breathe deeply, breathe slowly. You can breathe through anything.

Breathing slows down our minds and bodies. It allows us to clear out anxiety and dread. By following our breath, we can journey to that calm, inner place of ourselves.

So, we are all called to sit and breathe. Sitting and breathing allows the time to imagine, to dream, to conceive of ourselves and our world in new ways, and to birth the action that brings those dreams into the world.

What are you called to imagine, to dream, to breathe into your life? What are you called to breathe out of your life?

Find time in your life to just breathe.

Action is the counterpart to breath. Be in the world. 2

Breathing is, by itself, not enough.
By being born into a physical body, we are called to be in and of this world while at the same time maintaining spirit.

Take those images, dreams and conceptions that have come to you through your breathing into action. What steps can you take that will bring them to reality in your life and the lives of others? How do you take these actions in a heartful and joyful way so that you bring light and peace into the world?

Find time for action in your life.

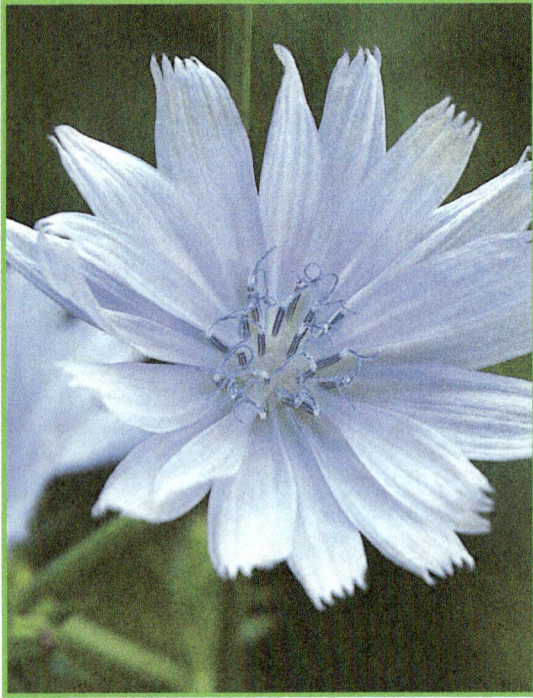

3 Invite the Great Mother into your heart.

Just as the ocean's tides are constant, the Great Mother is always with you. Just as there is a masculine principal in the world, the Universe, and the metaphysical plane, there is a feminine heart in all things. Think of all the things in this world that have co-creators, co-generators. The Great Mother has imagined and nourished you into being. Bring her into your life. She has the gifts of creativity, fecundity, nurturing, and art, among others, to give you. She wants you to accept them and use them for yourself and others.

Open your heart to her, invite her in, and accept the gifts that she has to give you. What are the particular and special gifts that she has just for you? Remember, you are never alone as long as she resides in your heart.

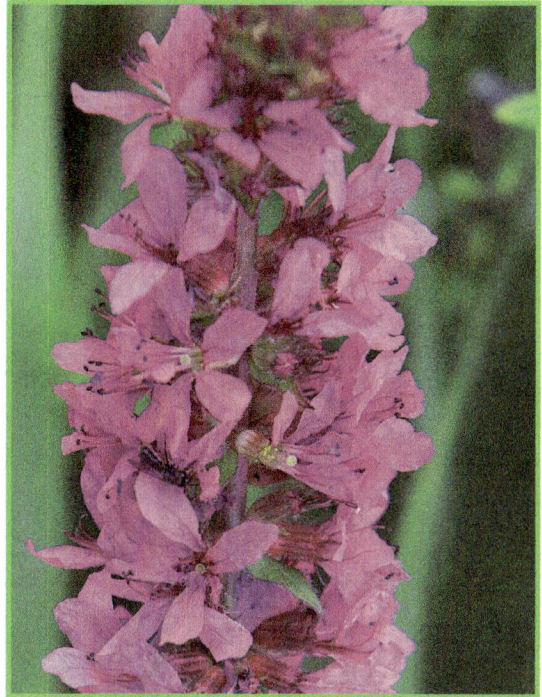

Invite the Great Father into your heart. 4

Just as the sun rises every day, the Great Father is always with you. While inviting the Great Mother into our hearts, we need to remember that the Great Father is her co-creator. While remembering her, we should not abandon him. He has many gifts to give us as well: the gifts of right action, clear speaking, and being grounded in the world and your physical self, among others. He wants you to accept these gifts as your own and use them well and thoughtfully for yourself and others.

Open your heart to him, invite him in and accept the gifts that he has to give you. What are the particular and special gifts that he has just for you? Remember, you are never alone as long as he resides in your heart.

5 The Holy Spirit invites you to live your heart in the world.

We often think of spirit as solely a thing of the metaphysical plane; however, our spirit is what we put out into the world, the love that we hold in our soul that makes us who we are in the world. Thus, while the Holy Spirit is of the Great Mother and Father, the Holy Spirit, creating that duality of world/spirit, wants our heart to be in the world. By having your heart in the world, it means that you look at living, at action, at existing in a way that creates love, light, compassion, and generosity. It is for this reason that the Holy Spirit invites you to live your heart in the world and not solely in the inner space of your being.

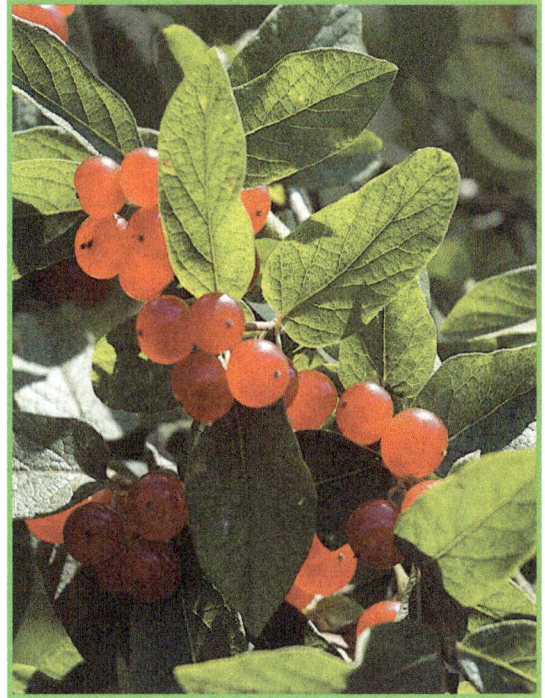

Holy Wisdom invites you to enter your deepest self. 6

The ancient knowledge that is being remembered, that is coming back into the world, resides in your deepest self. The knowledge that you need to exist in the world in the new/old way is there in your deepest inner self. The seeds of love, light, compassion, and generosity dwell there in that place where we have banished them so that we could live in the way called for by the times between the old and the new. Delve as deeply as you need to find the seeds of this wisdom, plant those seeds, nourish them, water them, and harvest the result. It is for this reason that Holy Wisdom invites you to enter your deepest self.

7   Live in your blood and bones.

Over time, a number of cultures, societies, and religions have asked us to forget about our bodies; they have made the physical inferior to the spirit/soul. The body has even been made sinful in some cases. The truth is our bodies are neither inferior to the spirit/soul nor are they sinful. And, in fact, our blood and bones contain wisdom if we listen to them. Feel the blood pulse. What does your body tell you when you are trying to make a particular decision or are faced with a situation or problem? Do you feel fit and well? Do you feel your heart race? Do you feel nauseous? Where do these feelings come from—your body or your mind? Listen to what they have to tell you and honor them.

Live in your breath. 8

Breath sustains us as physical beings, but breath is also a thing of the spirit, the soul. It can help connect us to the inner space. While reclaiming our physical selves and knowledge, we need to remain in touch with our breath. It has knowledge as well. What does your breath tell you? Is your breathing calm and even? Are you gulping air or having some other difficulty breathing? Is how you are breathing at a particular moment related to your physical, emotional, or spiritual health? Is it related to one or all of them? Listen to what your breath has to tell you and honor it.

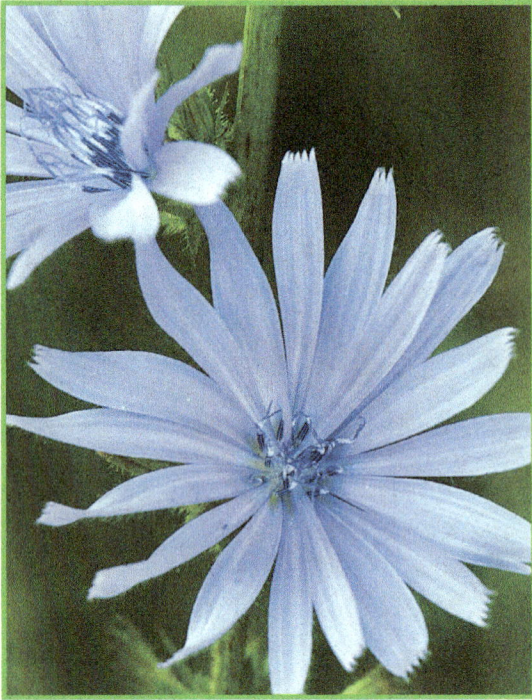

9 The Heart is a receptor.

The heart, meaning your physical heart as well as your heart center and heart chakra, is a receptor. The blood that sustains us flows into it. But the combined heart also receives knowledge. It can receive, if we are open to it, the love and compassion that others have for us. Have you ever said to yourself or someone else that you know something in your heart? This is not just a metaphor—we do know things in our heart. The heart is an energetic receptor. What do you want your heart to receive? What can you do to help your heart receive what you want to enter it?

The Heart is a transmitter. 10

The heart, meaning your physical heart as well as your heart center and heart chakra, transmits. The blood that sustains us flows out of it. But the combined heart also sends out love and compassion, as well as knowledge and wisdom. What thoughts, ideas and feelings do you send out into the world? They all have an energetic effect—on you and on others. Do they create the effect that you desire? What is your heart transmitting? What can you do so that your heart transmits only the things that you want it to?

11 Time does not exist in the heart of the universe. Be there.

Science tells us that there is no literal heart of the universe; however, whenever you dive deeply enough into your inner self, you know the heart of all things. This heart is the all-encompassing love, knowledge and wisdom that we seek, and, when we arrive in that heart, time does not exist—all is flow, all is stopped—all at the same time. It is in this "heart" of the universe that we come to know the healing of that love, compassion and knowledge as well as our deepest soul existence. Find your way there.

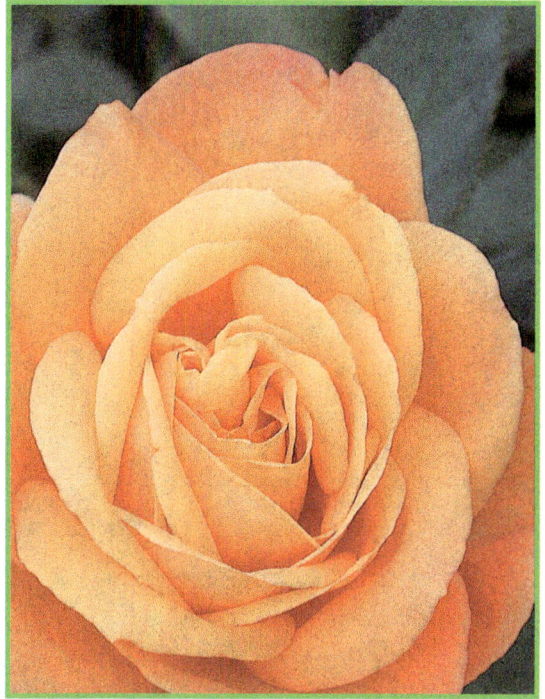

Time exists on the human plane.
Be here.

12

While it would be wonderful to exist in the bliss of the heart of all things at all times, each of us exists in a physical body. This body must eat, sleep, exercise, think, earn a living, and do all the things that human life calls us to do and be. Many believe that we have made an agreement as to what we are to learn and accomplish when we are born to this life. If we spend all our time in the heart of the universe, we fail to live fully in our physical bodies, as well as failing to accomplish what we are called to do here. Find your way here.

13 There is an **Edge** between you and the universe.

Where and what is your Edge? What is between it and you? Where do you begin and end? Is it your skin? Is it your mind? Is it the life that you live? Is it what makes you separate and distinct from others? People talk about pushing the envelope. Is your Edge the envelope? Does that envelope hold space for your thoughts and ideas, your love and compassion? Does it lead you? Do you lead it? Can you create anything without an Edge to hold the space for possibilities? Test for the Edge—see where and what it is, and then use it.

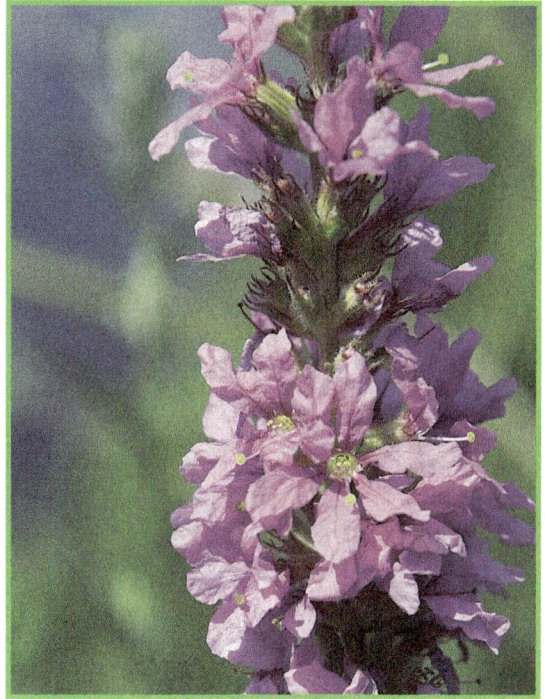

There is no Edge between you and the universe. 14

Science tells us that, despite what we perceive, the human body is mostly empty space. This is because the atoms of which we are composed are mostly empty space. Seemingly then, anything and everything can flow through us; everything can easily intermingle. Hence, there is no Edge between us and the universe. If so, what flows through from you to others, from others to you? What do you want this flow to consist of? Test for what flows through. Test to see if you can change what that is.

15 Life is a song. Sing it.

Everything in the universe has a frequency or harmonic at which it vibrates, including you and me. That means, in essence, each of us is a singing a song at all times—it is just one that we cannot necessarily hear with our ears. We can also learn to sing a song that can be heard at all times, if we choose. Can you find your frequency? What harmonic or tone resonates with you? What do you want your song to say about you? What do you want to sing?

Life is a school. Learn from it. 16

Many believe that part of each of our incarnations here is to learn specific lessons, or merely to remember Source. Even if that is not your belief, living seems to take constant learning—from the day-to-day tasks that come our way, to interacting with others, to lessons of the soul. What do you choose to learn? Being presented with all this wonderful knowledge is a gift. Accept this gift and use it.

17 Be open.

Life is change; change is life. New ideas and new ways of doing things come into being constantly. New technologies blossom and old ways come back into vogue. If we are closed, then we fail to grow and change; we fail to see alternative ways of acting and feeling. What can you change that would improve life? What should you retain?

Have boundaries. 18

Being open to change can be a marvelous thing, but, at the same time, you need to protect yourself. You need to have boundaries that say: "I will not let myself be exploited or act in ways that are not good for me. I will not exploit others or act in ways that are not good for others." What boundaries do you have in place? Are any missing? Are they protective boundaries or are they harmful boundaries?

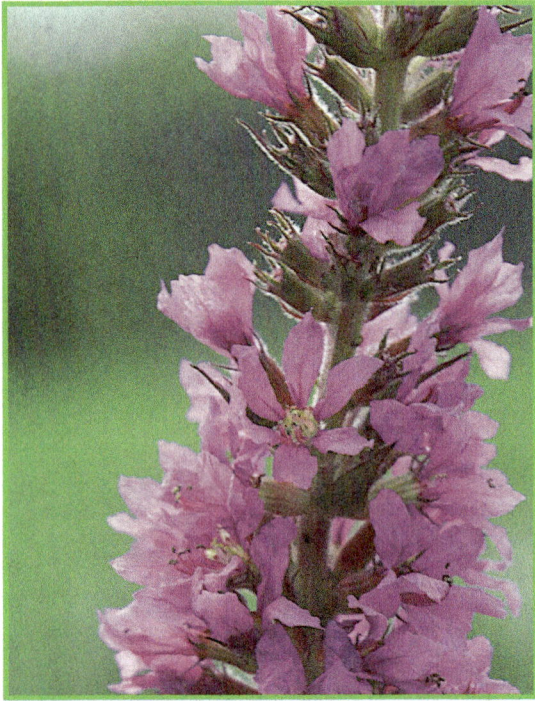

19 Go slowly. Take your time.

The old saying is take the time to stop and smell the roses. There is a great deal of sense in that, especially in this time of "hurry up, hurry up" that we see everywhere from debit card ads to the impatience of the person behind us in line at the grocery store. But rushing leads to errors, to rudeness, to hurt feelings. By going slowly and taking our time we can act in a mindful and heartful way—a way that speaks of peace and love in the world. Ask yourself, which way do I want to be? And, what can I do to be that way?

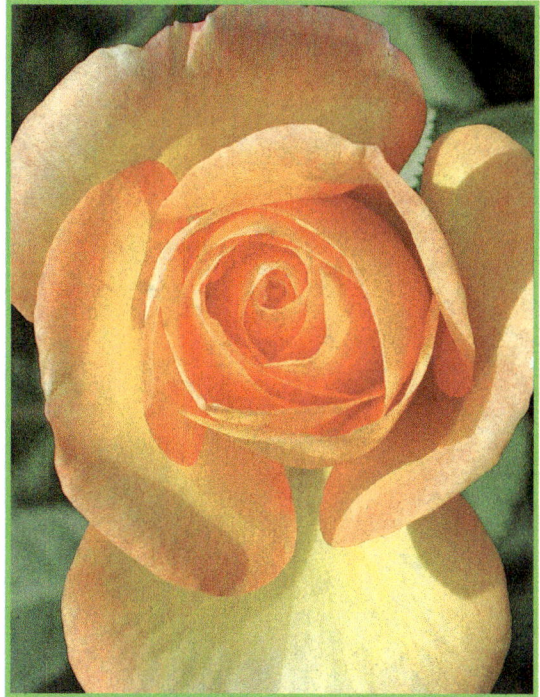

Embrace the swiftness of change. 20

Reclaiming acting in a mindful and heartful way is a wonderful thing. But, at the same time, that does not mean that change, in and of itself, should not be embraced, that keeping up with the swiftness of change is wrong. Change has brought us advances in many things. It is learning to determine what change you want to accept into your life that seems to be the key—change should neither be accepted nor rejected solely because it is change. How can you choose and accept change in a mindful and heartful way?

21 Love your country.

Loving your country does not mean loving your country right or wrong and blindly never questioning what it does. Your country does, however, deserve your love, care and concern, as does every person who lives in your country. It is where you were born or where you now live. You should desire the best for it and that it provides the best for itself and the world. What can we all do so that our country acts in the mindful and heartful way that we wish that all people would act? What can we do so that this love, care and concern extend to the plants and animals, the water, and the soil of our country?

What actions call out to you to show your love for your country?

Love the world. 22

Just as you are a citizen of a country, you exist in and are a citizen of the world. The world deserves the same love, care and concern that your country deserves. All the people in the world deserve that, as well as the plants, animals, waters and soils. This should be true if only on a selfish level, as what affects the world affects our country and ourselves. Hopefully, we are motivated in a mindful and heartful manner. What can we do to extend this to the world and everyone and everything in it?

What actions call out to you to show your love for the world?

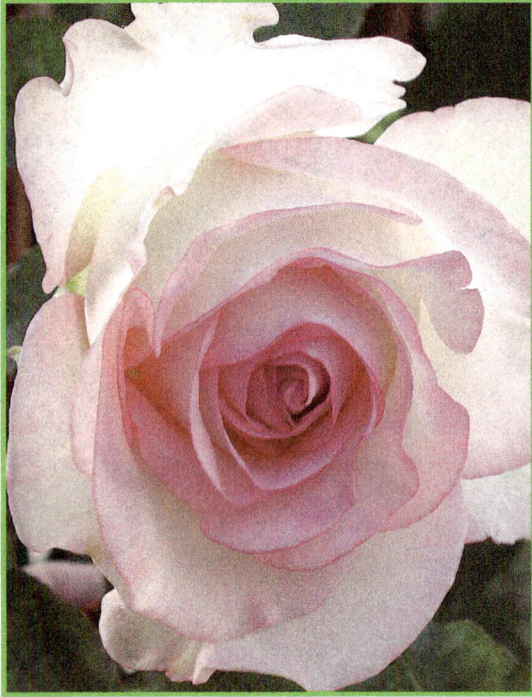

23 Accept that you are called to offer your best.

When I was growing up I knew that my parents expected me to do the best that I could—not better than I was capable of or less than I was capable of. I am not sure that this was articulated frequently, but I knew that they wanted me to do my best. I personally take the exhortation to do one's best to mean that you should always try to do the best work that you can, be the best friend that you can, keep your commitments as you can. It means that, to do your best, you need to acknowledge that doing your best is what is called for. Acknowledge this first, and then you can make your best effort to always do your best.

Accept that sometimes you will fail. 24

Just as we are called to do your best, we should also acknowledge that doing our best does not mean being perfect as humans define being perfect. There are things and forces that we cannot control. Other people may have input that changes the course of things or prevents us from accomplishing our best. And, in the eyes of the Universe, that is okay. We are allowed by the Universe to fail, as failure is a learning experience. And, this life is all about learning.

25 The universe is a quantum universe.

The universe is one of quarks, vast empty space, super strings, twinned electrons, and many other things that are, to us, invisible. Yet, these invisible things create and hold together the universe and all life in it. The quantum universe is, to many of us, mysterious and holds the possibility of miracles and wondrous events. It is a universe where the observer changes the observed, of chaos theory, and the like.

Can the contemplation of the quantum aspect of the universe spark your imagination? Is the idea of the quantum overwhelming? Does it sparkle with possibilities? Where can this contemplation of infinite possibilities lead you?

The universe is a Newtonian universe. 26

How many of us have heard of the Newton watching the falling apple? I use the term Newtonian because of this familiar myth and the images it helps create about physics. The macrocosmic aspect of the universe can be found in Newtonian physics, and in the physics of many others. The universe contains the large, the concrete, and the seemingly determinate and set—rules where things always work the same way.

What can contemplation of the Newtonian universe tell us? Although seemingly set and not changing, how can it help us to find our way?

27 Embrace the Feminine.

For far too long, the feminine principle has been rejected and repudiated, devalued and discarded. By the feminine principle, I mean the creative, the intuitive and the nurturing, and not the definition of feminine meaning limited to females and those things that are stereotypically female, although the female has been rejected as well. How do you define the feminine aspect of Source and the Universe? What of all the possible things that can be defined as feminine, do you wish to embrace, to make a part of yourself and your world?

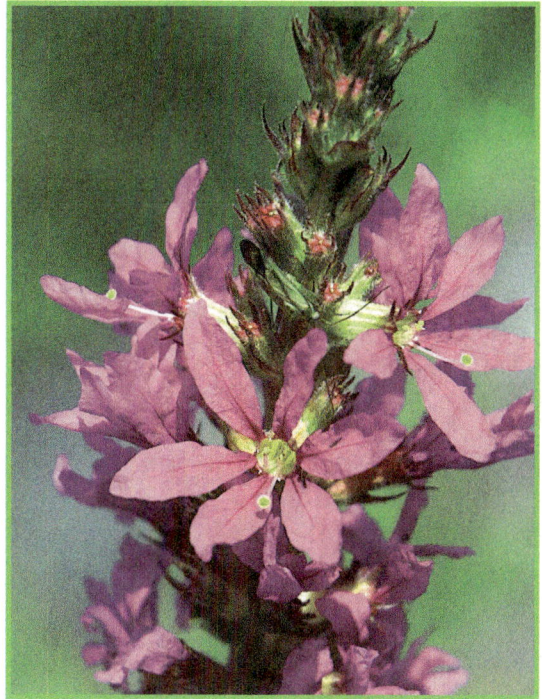

Embrace the Masculine. 28

Just because we need to bring the feminine back into the world to restore balance does not mean that we should categorically reject the masculine. I do not mean the stereotypic macho, swaggering aspect of men. I mean the strength and analytic skill that arises out of the true masculine. How do you define the masculine aspect of Source and the Universe? What of all the possible things that can be defined as masculine, do you wish to embrace, to make a part of yourself and your world?

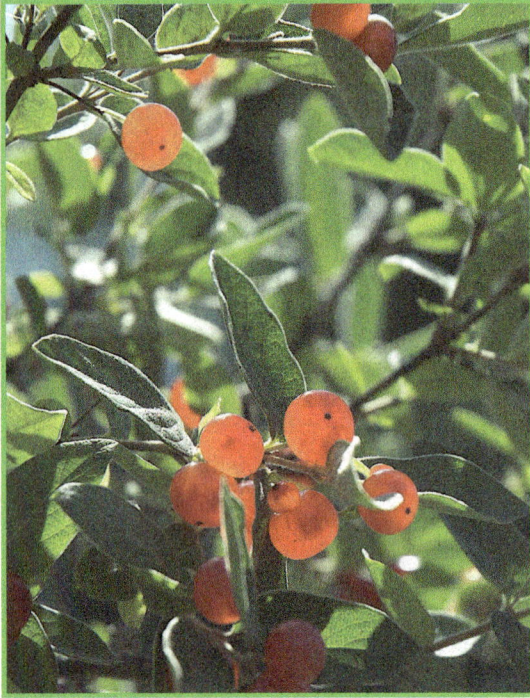

29   Clouds exist on sunny days.

If we could live in bliss at all times, everything might appear to be sunlight and illuminated at all times. For most of us, however, life is not lived in a state of continual bliss. Bliss may visit and then leave. There are some to whom bliss never comes. And, even for the most spiritually adept, life can be troublesome. It is how we react to the difficult that is the test. How do you deal with difficult situations or people, or with injustice? Is this how you want to continue to move through life? If not, what do you want to change about how you react to the clouds in your life? What steps can you take to make the changes that you want to make?

Bright starlight illuminates the darkest nights. 30

St. John of the Cross wrote of the dark night of the soul. This comes to many. And, even if you are never visited by this dark night, you have the literal dark night each and every day, as well as the dark night of troubles that come and seem to overwhelm. But, if we breathe deeply and look closely, the bright starlight peeks through, even through the clouds and the haze of living. It can be hard to see the actual stars in an urban area, but look carefully and you will find some. Look through the dark night of life to find the illumination. What can you do to achieve this?

31 Dance your body through life.

We are physical bodies and not just souls. Our physicality and what it offers us needs to be honored. One way to do that is to move in some way: to dance, to twirl, to jump, to leap, to stroll, to run, or to do whatever your body tells you it needs to do. We do not feel as well, do not "work" as well, if we do not move.

What is your way to dance through life?

Rest your mind in the One. 32

While our bodies need to move, our bodies and our minds need to rest. One way to rest is to rest your mind in the One, Source, and the Center of all things. You can pray, meditate, contemplate, look at beautiful scenery, listen to beautiful music, visit the ocean, read great poetry—whatever your mind tells you it needs to do.

What is your way to rest your mind in the One?

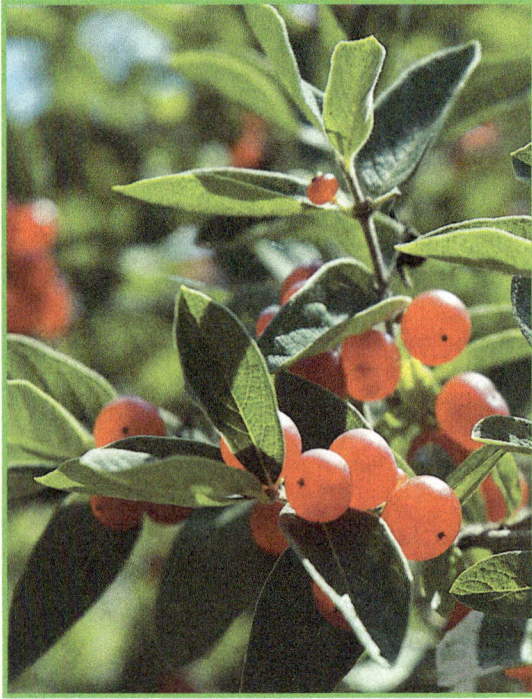

33   It is said that...

We frequently listen to what others say about life, love and the universe, but often without critical thinking. It is not that we should ignore what others say, but rather that we should judge for ourselves the validity of what we are being told. There can be much value in what others say—just as a lot of what others say has no bearing on our own lives. The point is to hear what others say, think clearly about it, and chose for ourselves what we wish to incorporate into our lives and belief systems.

What can you do to help yourself think critically, to learn what resonates, what has value?

I know that... 34

Knowledge comes to us in many ways—reading, listening to speeches and sermons, and watching television. We say to ourselves: "I know this; I know that." And, we truly do know things. But, do we know them in our bones; do we know them from resonance with the Universe?

How do you know things? Where does your knowledge come from? What comes from your deepest, inner self? Does it have more worth than what you learn externally? How do you know?

We need that deep, inner knowledge to balance out what we know from external sources. What can you do to help yourself learn from this source?

35 Accept and use what ancient wisdom has to give us.

Ancient wisdom, which flows down to us through the centuries, is the things of the heart and spirit that ring true, that work no matter the current state of thought or technology. Not all old things are of ancient wisdom, so you must sort and sift carefully to discern what ancient wisdom has to give us. Once you find it, then you can use it.

What can you do to find ancient wisdom? How will you know it when you find it? To what use can you put it?

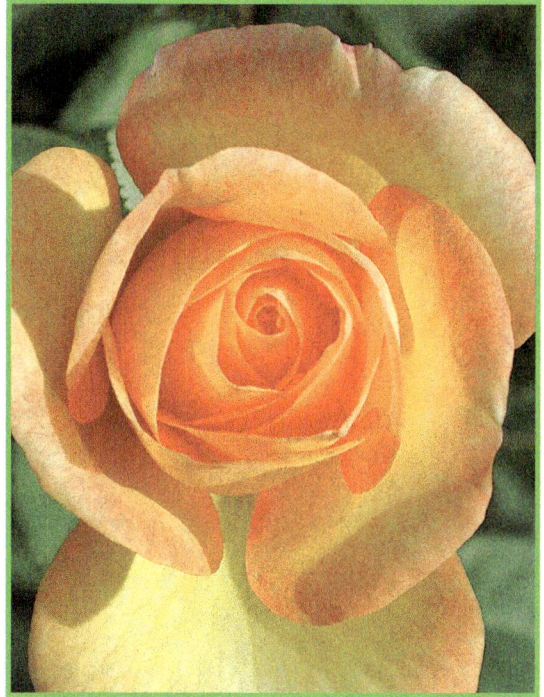

Modern wisdom has much to offer. Use It. 36

Seeking out ancient wisdom to use today does not mean that we should categorically reject modern wisdom. Not all wisdom was revealed in ancient times, some comes slowly as it is needed. New wisdom builds on the old, the ancient. But not all new knowledge or technology should be embraced by everyone or in all situations.

What can you do to distinguish what is new wisdom to be used from new knowledge that is not something to be incorporated into your life?

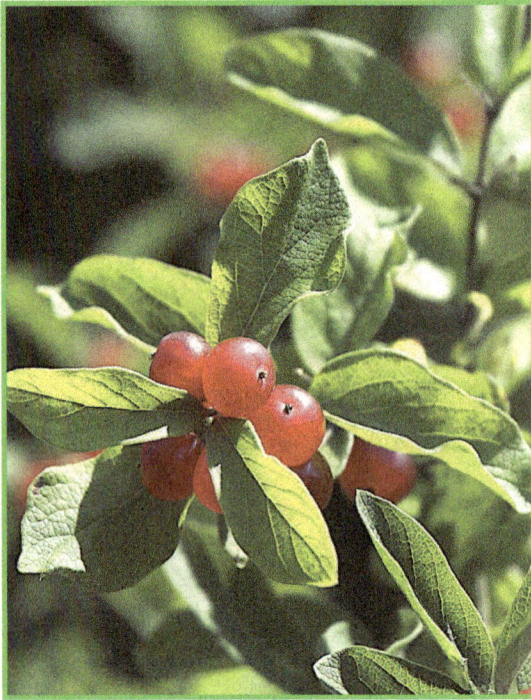

37 It is good to plan and prepare.

There are times in life when we need a roadmap to tell us how to get where we are going; when we need schedules to tell us when to leave and arrive; when we need lists of things to do. Moving through our physical life merely on trust that it will all work out, that what we want will come, is thought without action, without doing the work required of us.

When do you need your roadmap, your schedules, and your lists? Which of all of these are the ones that you should use?

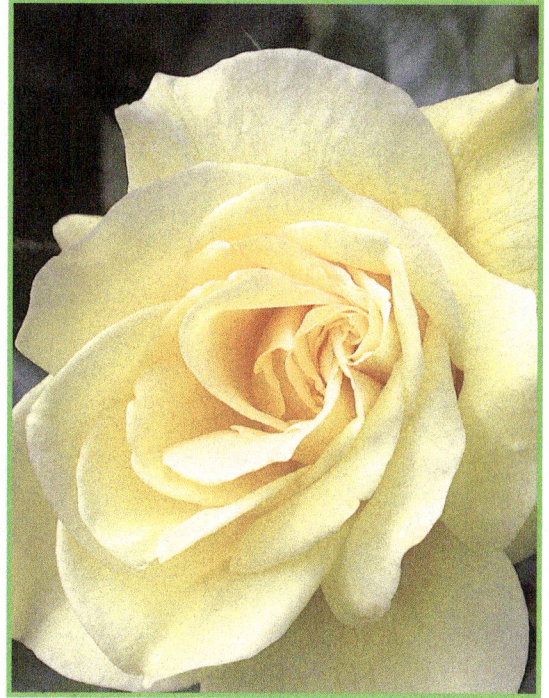

It is necessary to be spontaneous. 38

While we do need to plan and prepare to move successfully through our physical lives, we also need to know when to follow that whisper in our ear to travel the side road, to stop and play, to take the opportunity to do nothing.

What is the counterpart in your life for busyness, for overbooking yourself, for what keeps you from working on your deepest inner self?

39 The earth is magnificent.
Enjoy it. Take care of it.

The earth is our home, our Mother. It feeds us. It provides us a place to live. It provides things of beauty for us to enjoy, others to interact with.

Be outdoors. Interact with the Mother just as you interact with your family and friends. Take care of her.

What can you do to accomplish this? What about the earth calls to you?

The world of the spirit is glorious. Enjoy it. Take care of it.

40

The world of the spirit exits in the same place and time as the world of the earth. They are intertwined. The world of the spirit needs to be enjoyed along with the world of the earth for both to thrive. Love, laughter and joy make up the world of the spirit.

What brings you love, laughter and joy? What calls to you, makes you happy? See this as part of your work.

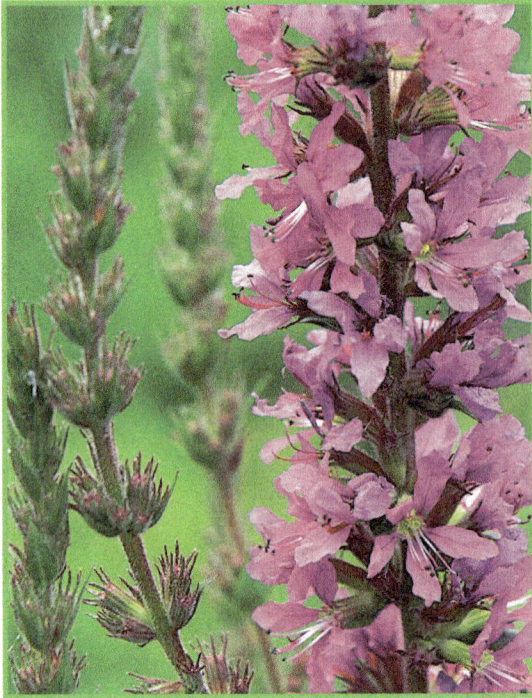

41 Let the nature of the Elements support you in your journey.

The Elements, also called earth, air, fire, and water, each have symbolic meanings. Earth is stable, solid. Air is breath, life, song. Fire is passion, compassion and the burning away of what is not needed. Water flows and nourishes. They also have specific correspondences in different cultures with the four directions and with spiritual development, among other things.

Which of these things is missing in your life? Which one of the elements calls to you, saying I have much to teach you? What can you study and use from each of these elements that will help you on your journey in this life?

Let the nature of Mind guide you in your journey. 42

What is meant by "Mind" here? Is it your individual mind or the Universal Mind? If you take on a connectedness to the nature of the Universal Mind, you can tap into the wisdom of the One, the wisdom of the ages, and the wisdom of now.

This connectedness, if allowed to grow and flourish, will help guide you on your path in this life. What can you do to create and nurture this connection?

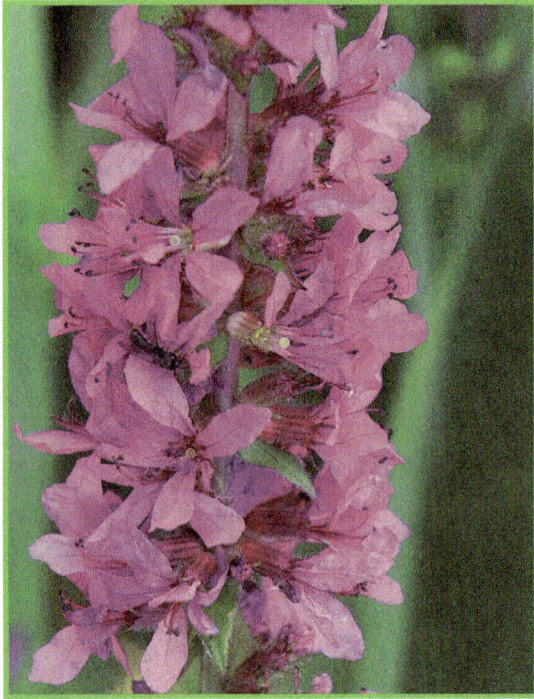

43 What you want.

For many of us, we want what we want and we want it NOW. And, much of what we want seems to be material with a mixture of the spiritual. If you were to make a list of all the things that you want, it could be a very long list, encompassing things from the trivial to the profound. Which of those things on your list can you say yes to if you ask about each one: Will this make my life better? If so, how? Will this help me grow my spirit? If so, how? What does asking these questions do to the list of what you want?

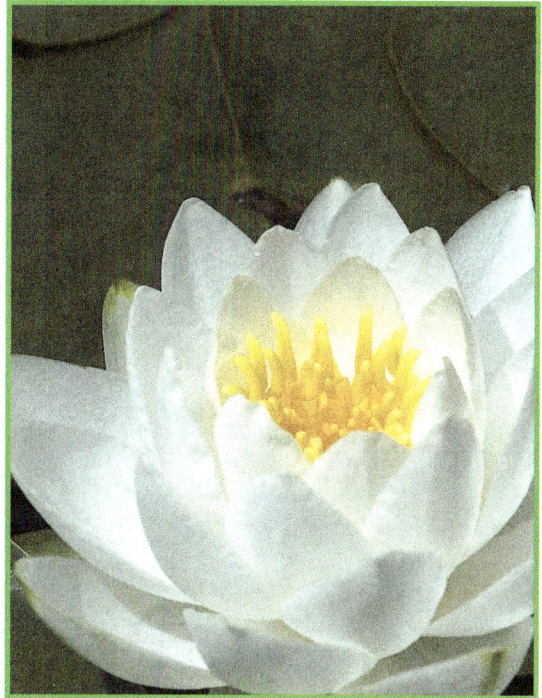

What you need. 44

Just as we can have a long list of what we want, we can have a long list of what we think we need. We do need clean air and water, nourishing food, clothing, and a decent, safe, affordable home. We need work to provide income, and, for many of us, work of the spirit. Family and friends most likely should be on everyone's list. After these, what do you truly need? If you were to make a list, the questions would be: Why do I need this thing? What difference will it make to my life if I do not have this thing that I think that I need?

45 Be playful.

No matter our age, we need moments of fun, moments of joy and laughter. Play can bring these into our lives.

How do you define being playful? What is play for you? How much do you have in your life? If you need more, what can you do to bring playfulness into your life?

Be mindful. 46

While bringing play into our lives, we should not banish being mindful. Being mindful is taking that few seconds to think before speaking out in anger, to acknowledge our sorrow at hurting others, and to consider the consequences that our actions have for ourselves and others. It means having the intent that all we do and say is for the highest and best good for all.

What steps can you take to start on a more mindful path?

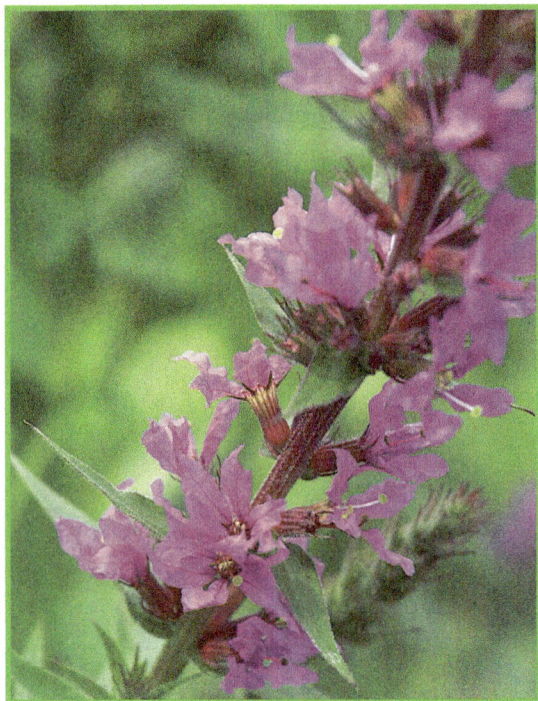

47 Nurture.

The old debate is about whether nurture or nature has the most importance in a person's development. The truth is that they are equally important.

Nurture means the providing of sustenance, the act of bringing up, educating, and helping growth and development. What in the way of nurturance have others given you? What have you given yourself? What are you giving others? What do you and others need now, even in adulthood?

Nature. 48

The old debate is about whether nurture or nature has the most importance in a person's development. The truth is that they are equally important.

What has nature given you? Where do you come from? What do you come from? What gifts has this given you? What about this can you use now on your path?

49 In the eyes of the Universe, at this moment, you are perfect for who you are.

An entity by the name of O'Brien once said to me: "In the eyes of the Universe, at this moment, you are perfect for who you are." Knowing this fact is quite liberating, because it says that the Universe does not expect us to be other than who we are at any particular moment. At any particular time, you are called only to be the best you that you can be for your path at that moment.

Who are you at this moment? What is the best you that you can be at this moment? Can you allow yourself this gift?

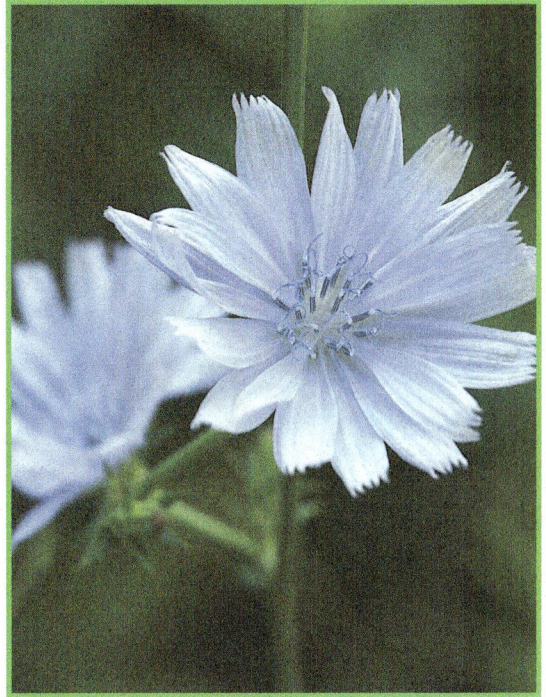

Do not stand still. Do not be static. Grow. Heal. Change. 50

While the Universe, at any particular moment, sees us as perfect for who we are, it wishes that we move, grow, change, and heal so that we can continue to be the best we can be. This is because, as I believe, part of our path here on earth is growth, healing and change.

What can you do to not be static, to grow, to change, and to heal? What do you need to bring into your life to do this?

51 You are the Beloved.

The One has created you. The One is infinite love, and, therefore, you are the Beloved of the One. This is the main piece of knowledge in your heart. Accept it. Acknowledge it.

In what ways can you fully live with this knowledge? What can you do to wholly accept, integrate and acknowledge this fact?

You are the one called to love. 52

You have been given the great gift of being the Beloved of the One. The acceptance of this gift by you, in turn, calls you to love. This love is the love of self, and the love of family and friends. It is the love of the stranger that creates compassion.

How can you live your life in love? What actions and thoughts create the love that you are called to bring into the world? What does this love look and feel like?

53 Compassion for others.

Part of the path of life is to learn to have compassion for others. Compassion helps us to grow, to change and to heal. We cannot as easily bring these things to others without first learning compassion.

What does compassion feel like? Does it have a sound, a taste, a color? How do you sense it? What can you do to help it blossom out into the world?

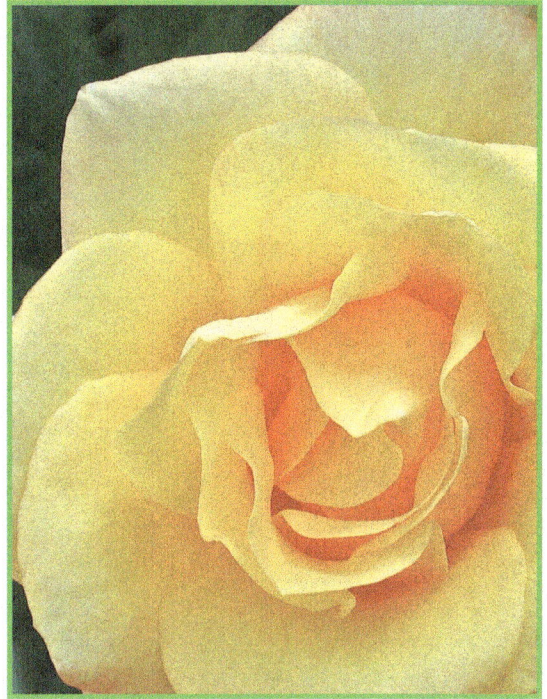

Compassion for yourself. 54

The wellspring of compassion is deep within ourselves. We create more and more compassion by giving it to ourselves, and then by giving it to others. Nurture compassion for yourself first because you cannot as easily give it to others if you do not give it to yourself. After all, how will you recognize compassion for others if you do not recognize it for yourself?

In what ways can you nurture compassion for yourself? What can you do to know it when you "see it?"

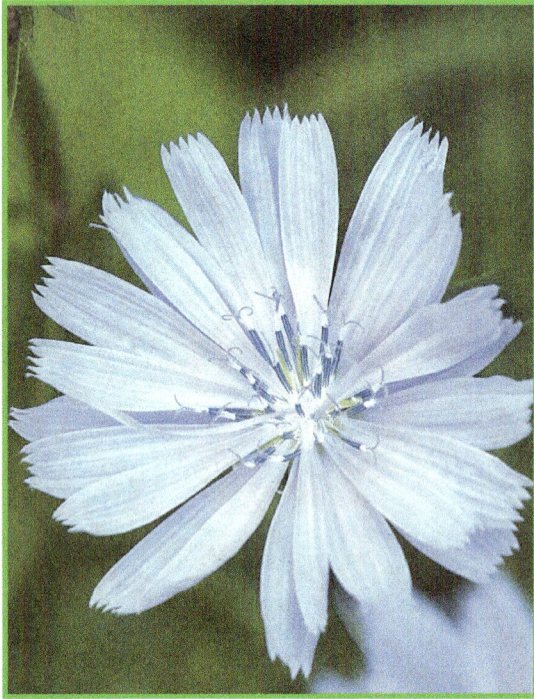

55   Let it all go. It will come when it wants to.

This does not mean that you should not envision what you want and need coming into your life. It does not mean that you should not do the work to make these things happen. What it means is that you should detach from the emotions of desperation and having to have something NOW. Things will not come without envisioning and work, but emotional attachment to an outcome will not necessarily make things happen on our time schedule or exactly in the form that we want them to occur.

What does letting go mean to you? What does it feel like? What can you do to let go, while at the same time working to bring things into being?

Seek it. Seek it in yourself. 56

Things cannot happen without our first looking inward to see what we feel called to bring into fruition without checking to see if something is a need, a want, or something we think we have to do. At about the time that I wrote this, I realized that a project that I had been trying to bring into fruition was one that I thought I was supposed to do. It turns out that I did not seek carefully enough inside myself. Thus, I am letting it go so as to bring my energies to some things that I am really called to do.

What can you do to seek it in yourself? Meditate? Pray? Read? Sing? Dance? And, what is "it" for you?

Exercises

Instructions for Part 3

Please choose some meditative music to play while doing the exercises. The meditation period for each exercise should be between five and ten minutes unless noted otherwise. If working in a group, please try to be respectful of the others in the group as to the amount of time in meditation, in journaling, and in talking about your experience with each exercise.

I believe it is important to do the Preparation for the Work section at the beginning of each session as well as the Three Questions exercise after each session, whether you do all of the exercises at once, you do only two or three of the exercises at a time, or if you decide to repeat an exercise or two over time. Doing the Three Questions exercise will help you track the shift occurring in you that doing the work helps create.

The directions for the exercise are at the beginning of this section. Blank pages are included in this section for you to record what you received during doing an exercise. You can write, draw and/or collage to record whatever you feel the need to document. There are two exercises where you are directed to specifically to draw. You can then write or collage afterwards if you feel called to do so. However, if drawing is more your medium, then, by all means draw after all the exercises rather than writing.

The last exercise in this section is called The Three Questions. It purposefully does not ask you to journal about your experience. This exercise is meant as a brief check-in with yourself. Doing this exercise over time and writing the answers sequentially can help you keep track of your transformation.

The Preparation for Work, The Six Directions, and the Three Questions exercises do not involve picking one of the meditation images. There are specific instructions for these exercises. You will always use image number 44 for the Four Elements exercise, 31 for the Dance Your Body through Life exercise, images number 25 and/or 26 for the Connecting to the Energy of the Universe exercise, and image 51 for the I Am of Value Exercise. The Dance Your Body through Life exercise should be done about halfway through the exercises you choose to this exercise as it is meant to help you ground yourself.

For all the other exercises, pick a meditation image at random. Meditate on that one image while listening to the music you have chosen to play. You can also choose to read and contemplate the meditation in the book while going into meditation, or look at it after you have finished the exercise.

If you are working on this in a group, please allow time for each person to discuss what was received. I hope that groups will create a safe space that allows everyone to share or not share. Once you have completed the meditations, journal, draw and/or collage what you have seen, felt or heard during the meditation. Pages are included for you to record your experience.

Preparation for Work

Play some appropriate meditation music, and then chant Om or another mantra with the intent to open up the heart center and the throat chakra. Opening the heart center helps you connect to the Universe and to yourself. Opening the throat chakra helps you speak your truth and will help prepare you to receive and then journal what you experience during the mediations that follow. You can journal if you receive some information during this preparatory work, but it is not necessary to do so.

This exercise should last about two to three minutes. You may spontaneously end together when working in a group.

The Four Elements/The Six Directions

The Four Elements and the Six Directions are guided meditations that continue the preparatory work begun in the previous section. Choose to do either the Four Elements or the Six Directions using appropriate meditation music; it is not necessary to do both.

Read the directions for the meditation that you have chosen. Once you have done the meditation, journal what you received.

The Four Elements

Find meditation image number 41. Sit and breathe deeply to the music while meditating on the image for a few minutes as a gate into your heart. Close your eyes and see yourself in a beautiful meadow. The sky is blue and filled with puffy clouds. The sun is shining brightly with a slight breeze blowing. As you look around, you see a smiling figure, who is your guide for this meditation, welcoming you to sit. Your guide tells you which element—earth, air, fire, or water—is providing you information today.

Sit with your guide and listen to the information that your guide has to tell you—what you need to learn from that element.

When your time with you guide is done, thank your guide for the help and information, and then slowly return from the meditation.

Journal about your experience with your guide.

The Six Directions

Sit and breathe deeply to the music. Close your eyes and see yourself in a forest glade. The wind is blowing gently, sunshine dapples through the trees, and you hear a stream flowing nearby. As you look around, you see six paths radiating away from the center of the glade. You see a light shining down one of the paths—it calls to you and you follow it into the forest. As you enter the path, you see a small stone pillar with the word north, east, south, west, above, or below carved into it. You note this and walk down the path. You come to another glade where a guide is waiting for you. You sit with the guide of this direction, who imparts to you the information that you need to learn from this direction.

When your time with your guide is done, thank your guide for its help and information, and then slowly return from the meditation.

Journal about your experience with this guide.

See a Number

Go into meditation asking to see or be told a number from 1 through 56. When you have the meditation image with that number in front of you, meditate on the image. Then journal what you received.

My Heart's Story

Pick an image and go into meditation. Using the chosen image and text as an opening into your heart, ask your heart what its story is. Write your heart's story in a paragraph or two.

You can choose to journal about this experience or let your heart's story speak for itself.

Partnering

This exercise will be done only when working in a group. Pair up with someone in the group. Each person in the pair chooses an image and meditates on it for a few minutes. Then, sitting knee to knee, take turns telling each other what came out of your deepest self. Then each of you tells your partner what you sensed or felt about what you were told. You may journal about this if you wish.

What Lives in My Heart

Pick a card and go into meditation to see what lives in your heart as shown to you by meditating on the image.

This time, instead of writing, draw a heart shape on a page following this exercise, then draw, write, or collage what you saw and felt using the heart as a frame—even breaking through the frame if you feel called to do so. You can also journal about the meditation on a different page.

Dance Your Body through Life

This exercise, of course, may be done even if you are only doing a few of the exercises; however, it should be done about half way through a session if you are doing all of the exercises in Opening the Heart.

To do this exercise, meditate on image 31 for a short time. Play some music that is a bit livelier than the mediation music that you have been using. Now, dance, twirl, sway, or do whatever your body wants to do. This exercise is designed to help bring you back into your body for the rest of the exercises. Do this as long as your body feels the need.

There are pages provided to journal about the experience, but it is not necessary. The purpose of this exercise is to reconnect you with your body and to ground you for continued work.

Connecting to the Energy of the Universe

Go into meditation using image 25 and/or image 26 to see the energy of the universe as shown by meditating on one or both. See how you are connected to this energy.

This time, instead of writing, draw what you were shown during your meditation. You can then, if you choose, write or collage what you saw, what you felt on this picture. You can also use a different page to journal about your meditation experience.

Stream of Consciousness

Pick a meditation image, and this time, instead of meditating on the image *just start writing without thinking* about whatever is triggered by the text portion of the image. Once you have finished your stream of consciousness writing you can journal, if you choose, about what you experienced during this exercise. *This exercise is about letting go*.

Tell a Story

Pick an image and meditate on it. Then, using the text on the card as the first sentence, write a story of a paragraph or two in length. Unlike the stream of consciousness writing exercise, this writing exercise should be conducted in a thoughtful and purposeful way.

This story should be a different story than the one you received during the Heart's Story exercise. It should also be different from what you wrote during the stream of consciousness exercise.

You can choose to journal about the experience afterwards.

Tell a Story II

This is a variation of the Tell a Story exercise. This time randomly pick three meditation images. Contemplate each one briefly. Please do not be concerned about whether the three together make sense, just spend some time meditating on the three moving back and forth between them as you feel called to do to meditative music. Write a story beginning with the first image picked, then the second one and finally the third.

You can journal about this afterwards if you choose.

What Energy Blocks Exist in Me?

Pick a meditation image and go into meditation using the image to assist you in finding one or more energy blocks inside you. You will find an energy block in different ways. It might just announce itself—in essence it might say something such as "Yoo-hoo, I am over here," or you may feel as if something is dammed up in your energy flow. It will feel sluggish, slow, or on occasion, completely blocked. If there is more than one, you will certainly want to work with only one at a time during a session.

Once you have found an energy block to work with, ask yourself if it has a texture, a color, an odor, a shape, etc. Once you have this in mind, ask the energy block why it was created, does it have a name, and then, what does it need to transform into positive healing energy? Work with the energy block toward this change. You can ask it if it has a new name when you perceive a shift in the energy block. You should note any changes in color, texture, odor, or shape. You might need to work with an energy block more than once.

You can then journal, draw, and/or collage about this experience.

I Am of Value

Go to image 51 and meditate on it using it to go into your heart. Open your inner ear and ask your heart, "What is of value about me?" or "How am I valued?" List all the things that your heart has told you. You can list them as you receive them, or you can list them after the meditation is over.

You can, of course, choose to journal, draw, and/ or collage about this experience as well.

The Three Questions

Play meditation music of your choosing. Turn to the next page; ask yourself the question on that page and journal the answer. Then do the questions on the next two pages in the same manner. You should answer the questions quickly with the answers coming deep from in your heart. Don't ponder the questions, *just answer them immediately*. This exercise is not intended to be an in-depth writing experience. It is intended to be immediate, to be accomplished swiftly.

Who am I?

What am I?

Where am I?

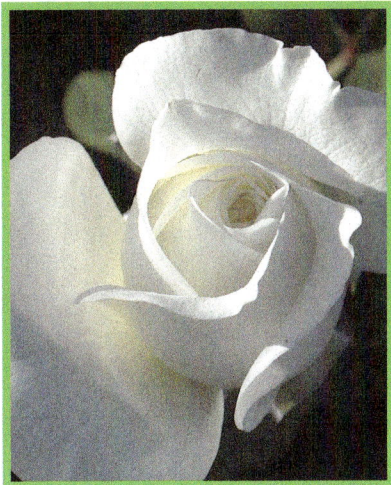

Notes

Acknowledgements

I gratefully acknowledge the many people who have been cheerleaders during this process, but I want to especially acknowledge those who have provided pivotal ideas or sustaining help. These are:

Massage/reiki therapist Rochelle Delacroix for receiving and passing on the idea that I was to create a set of what she called "angel cards", an idea which evolved over time and resulted in the creation of *Opening the Heart*.

Intuitive adviser, Michael Traub and the entity he channels, O'Brien, for helping me evolve the idea provided by Rochelle into what is now called *Opening the Heart*, as well as telling me one day that in this moment I am perfect in the eyes of the universe.

Linda Lewis, the co-creator of the book, fellow seeker, and, who has from time to time, kept me going during the creation process with her laughter, her creativity and her warmth.

David Steiner, the photographer, for the lovely photographs used in this book, and for so graciously making me feel at home while I was working with Linda on *Opening the Heart*.

Ed Stevens, a designer, who was willing to meet with us and gave us his encouragement as well as his wise counsel.

Judie Yuill who gifted me with the concept of working with multiple meditation images at once.

Jennifer Comeau and Anne Fitzgerald for their concept of the Edge as taught in their workshop *An Exploration with Women at the Edge*.

James Wanless, author, keynote speaker, futurist, consultant, and creator of the *Voyager Tarot* and *Sustain Your Life* card sets for blessing *Opening the Heart* with a wonderful endorsement.

Dee Morris for using her keen eye in looking at *Opening the Heart* in its incarnation as a card set, which helped with refining the images.

The cheerleaders that I want to thank are: Barbara Moura, Carol McDermott, Amethyst Wyldfyre, Joan Cassidy, Claudette Paradis, and all those who have taken the *Opening the Heart* workshop and wished that they could take *Opening the Heart* home with them.

The concepts have come through me, but I sincerely believe that they were sent by my angels and guides, some of whom have been human guides. The Universe provides teachers and mentors in many different ways.

About the Author

Kathryn Samuelson was born and grew up in Illinois. She graduated from the University of Illinois College of Law and practiced law in Illinois for a little over 26 years. The Universe made it clear that it wanted her to move to Massachusetts. Once settled in Massachusetts, she realized that it was time to give up practicing law and begin her work as a psychic and life coach. She was gifted with the idea for *Opening the Heart: Meditations on How to Be* and asked to help bring it to fruition. Kathryn leads workshops based on *Opening the Heart*. She is a long time knitter, poet and meditator and has added mixed media art and beading to her creative repertoire. Kathryn is looking forward to the next adventure presented to her by the Universe. To find out more about Kathryn and her schedule visit www.kathrynsamuelson.com.